Some Assembly Required

Putting Together Your New Life in Christ

Fran & Jill Sciacca

World Wide Publications
A ministry of the Billy Graham Evangelistic Association
Minneapolis, Minnesota 55403

LIFELINES HINTS FOR LEADERS is a publication free
to all who request it. Write to: Lifelines, World Wide
Publications, 1303 Hennepin Ave., Minneapolis, MN 55403.

Some Assembly Required

World Wide Publications is the publishing ministry of the
Billy Graham Evangelistic Association.

Scripture quotations are taken from The Holy Bible, New International
Version. Copyright © 1973, 1978, 1984 International Bible Society.
Used by permission of Zondervan Bible Publishers.

ISBN: 0-89066-152-9

Printed in the United States of America

Why "Lifelines"?

Who in the world are Fran and Jill . . . is it Sky-Ocka??

The name "Sciacca" (actually pronounced "Shock-a") is probably not a familiar name to you. Let me take you on a quick trek through our lives, so you will know who we are and why we care so much about you.

Fran grew up in the shadow of older identical twin brothers who were football stars. While their photos and accomplishments appeared regularly in newspapers and magazines, Fran found himself wondering who he was besides "the twins' little brother." In high school, he decided to take his talents "elsewhere," completely out of the arena of athletics — he set out to become the best bass guitarist he could be. His rock band was a success, and soon Fran also made it to the pages of the newspaper. On one occasion, he played in front of five thousand people at a "battle of the bands" in Milwaukee, Wisconsin. Fame became Fran's total focus in his search for identity. He was popular at school and was elected class president for three years.

In college, Fran quickly blazed his way to the top of his fraternity. The professional status of his new rock group also gave him personal pride. The band's popularity soared beyond the college campus, and Fran began doing "warm-up" for nationally known entertainers such as Chase and B. J. Thomas. He had finally "arrived" — or so he thought. But why, he wondered, was the feeling of emptiness still lodged so deep in his soul?

Then in one year's time, the band began to break up, his girlfriend dumped him, and he received the devastating news that one of his brothers had been seriously wounded in the Vietnam War. It was as if someone had let the air out of his world. He felt alone in the universe. Even his twelve years of religious education in a private school didn't help him.

About this time, God brought a friend into Fran's life who had just committed his own life to Jesus Christ. Late one night in a quiet dorm room, Fran heard from him about the depth of God's love. For the first time, Fran had reason to believe that he was a valuable person, not because he was "cool," or a popular bass guitarist but because the God of the universe loved him and had paid the penalty for his sin. Fran found the identity he had always longed for in the person of Jesus Christ.

Jill's Journey

I grew up in "the suburbs," graduating with a class of more than seven hundred students. My years in high school could best be characterized by my quest to know, "Where's the party?" But when I was alone, I often thought about life and death — even suicide. I wrote poetry that exposed my inner fears, but felt they were "safe" as simple assignments for English class. As best I could, I squelched my spiritual emptiness by dancing, partying, working a little, and playing a lot.

My folly and flippant approach to study in high school forced me to be on probation for the first quarter of college. I buckled down to get good grades, but somehow managed to maintain my carefree lifestyle "to the max." I was dating a gifted art student, and together with other friends we embraced the sixties counter-culture. Our philosophy boasted that peace was possible; we could affect society and bring about lasting change. *We* were the answer to all of America's problems.

Yet in two years' time, I witnessed the tragic folly of the sixties philosophy in vivid detail. A best friend from high school had burned out on drugs. Another had died while on drugs. I had seen that our protests against the Vietnam War were leading to prison sentences. People were losing heart, dropping out. My boyfriend had been committed to a psychiatric ward in a hospital. My best girlfriend, who had entered college on a scholarship, had quit, disillusioned with life. My rock star heros had fallen from the thrones I'd placed them on. Jimi Hendrix had died. (I had been in the front rows at one of his concerts.) Jim Morrison was gone. Drugs and death seemed to go together. We were not the answer to America's woes — we were part of the problem!

So I fled from the fast lane and started studying philosophy, searching for answers but finding none. Finally, I desperately cried out to the God I had learned about in Sunday school as a child. I had always believed in him, but never realized that I could know him personally. Committing my life to him, I made him my Lord and found the peace I hadn't found in all my searching. I joined the ranks of the revival on our college campus, the one that had also swept Fran into the faith. We were radical, but now we had an anchor and a purpose that really was destined to succeed.

And Then, Fran & Jill

We were married after graduation from college. Our first home was in Wisconsin, out in the country, where we attended a small church. There we immediately gravitated to the youth. Three years and one son later, the Lord led us to Denver, Colorado, where Fran went to seminary. While in Denver, we were again drawn to teens as Fran did field work at a local church. Two years and another son later, the Lord led us to Colorado Springs Christian School, where Fran taught high-school Bible for several years. Now we also have the blessed bonus of twin daughters.

We needed to tell you all this for two reasons: First, everything that these studies deal with comes out of our own experience. Second, in many of the things that you're going to look at in *Lifelines: Getting a Hold on Life,* we totally "blew it." So not only do we understand the issues at hand, we also know the pain and temptation that go with the territory.

We believe that a genuine relationship with Jesus Christ and with those who are committed to him is the most fulfilling and exciting thing on this sometimes perplexing planet! We're not talking about people who "play church." We're talking about those who are really serious about falling in love with, and following, the One who died for us.

So be assured that your struggles are familiar to us. They are foes that we have fought too. They are battles that we often lost. But we know there is a way of victory, and we want to help you discover that door of hope.

We pray that, through a personal study of God's Word, you will gain a new vision for a meaningful life, walking with the Lord and living in victory.

Fran and I are a fun team. He is the architect; I am the builder. You will find the Bible study section of each chapter designed by Fran. I have helped Fran put a personal touch to the studies by telling a story you can relate to, about someone who has been a part of our lives. (Names, gender and nonessential details have been altered to protect the privacy of those involved.)

There is one more thing we want you to know as you begin this Bible study — we really care about you!

What Is "Lifelines"?

Life is tough! Being a teenager is even tougher. You bounce somewhere between adulthood and childhood, ping-ponging back and forth, not really landing on either side, never really knowing which side you're supposed to be on at any given moment. The temptation to give in or give up may seem greater than you can bear. You probably feel as if you're sinking in a sea of pressures and problems too deep and wide to navigate. Let's face it, life's a battle. But . . . on the other hand, is that so unusual?

What does it take to make the first-string soccer team? What's the cost of working your way to first-chair trumpet in the school band? How long did you have to practice to become the best guitarist at school? Remember those early morning practices for the spring play? It seems as if everything significant has a price tag. Maybe that's the way it's supposed to be; maybe that's the way God planned it. But he also provides the help we need along the way. *Lifelines: Getting a Hold on Life* is one of those helpers.

"Lifelines" Is Different.

Lifelines: Getting a Hold on Life is different. It won't help you "sail" through life, because nobody sails through life. But *Lifelines* will be honest with you about life, about God, about yourself, about your choices and your dreams. *Lifelines* promises to "put the cookies on the bottom shelf," to meet you right where you are and deal with the things that you have to deal with each day. It promises to provide answers where there are answers, and to ask questions where they need to be asked.

But, just as in the rest of life, there are some costs that go with these Bible studies. What are they? Simply this: *Lifelines: Getting a Hold on Life* promises to be honest with you, but you've got to be honest with yourself. And even more important — you've got to be honest with God. These studies are built on the presupposition that the Bible is God's Word. That means that your opinions and feelings have a genuine place in your life, but the final place is reserved for God's Word.

This Bible study cannot change your life; only God can do

that. But, God can't guide a parked car. You're the one who's got to cooperate with God as you carefully work through this study. You've got to be willing to let the Lord into your life, into your problems and pressures, into your battle. He wants to be beside you whether you are defeated or determined. If you are willing to pay this price, *Lifelines: Getting a Hold on Life* could very well be one of the most exciting things that happens to you this year.

Things to Keep in Mind:

Here are some important thoughts to keep in mind as you begin:

1. God is not a coach. He doesn't have a checklist for your performance. He loves you. In fact, he loves you just as you are as you begin this study.

2. Apply what you learn to yourself. Resist the urge to think of others who "really need to hear" what you are learning.

3. Be faithful. Whatever your commitment is, whether to a group or simply to yourself, keep it. Make it your goal to finish the study.

4. Be realistic. Weeds grow quickly, but an oak tree takes time. Look for small ways to grow. If you set goals that are too tough, you'll become discouraged. Small victories will encourage you to keep going.

Lifelines: Getting a Hold on Life accepts the fact that much of life is a battle for you. God wants you to win the battle. But remember: You can't have a victory where there's been no fight. You may fall — we all do — but learn to stand!

How to Use This Bible Study

This Bible study is part of a series entitled *Lifelines: Getting a Hold on Life*. Each study in the series centers around a single issue that you as a teenager face in the twentieth century. This study, *Some Assembly Required,* carries you into the world of your spiritual life. In particular, it deals with what you might call the basics of being a Christian — a sort of spiritual boot camp. In *Some Assembly Required* you'll find answers to questions such as: What changes can I expect to see in my life now that I am a Christian? What's the authority for my life? What is prayer, and how does God answer prayer?

In *Good News for a Bad News World* we likened the Christian life to a race. In this Bible study, you'll discover how to train for that race, how to be spiritually fit. Paul tells us in 1 Corinthians 9:24-25:

> Do you not know that in a race all the runners run, but only one gets the prize? Run in such a way as to get the prize. Everyone who competes in the games goes into strict training. They do it to get a crown that will not last; but we do it to get a crown that will last forever.

Jill and I have seen a lot of young people begin their relationship with God but "wash out" when they hit the college campus. Often, it is due more to neglect than giving up on God. *Some Assembly Required* won't make you a perfect Christian, because there's no such thing. But it *will* show you some basic truths about staying spiritually healthy that, if followed, will help you "run in such a way as to get the prize."

Each chapter of this study includes a real-life story, some personal study questions, and a summary discussion. Look for one major truth, a "Lifeline," as you go through each chapter. If there are specific things the study asks you to do, be sure to do them. The insights you pull out of these pages won't help you until you begin to put them into practice.

The only things you will need to complete this study are a Bible, a pen, and an open heart. We suggest that you use a version of the Bible that is easy to read, such as the *New International Version,* or *The Living Bible*. Make sure that your Bible has both the Old and New Testaments. You may also want to have a spiral notebook in which you can record thoughts and ideas that come to you while you study.

If you study *Some Assembly Required* in a group, you may find the optional group discussion questions in "The Bottom Line" section at the end of each chapter helpful. These questions are deliberately thought-provoking. You'll probably get more out of them if your youth pastor or group leader is present for the discussion.

There is another optional section near the end of each chapter entitled "His Lines." These are a few verses from the Bible that might be helpful as you seek to make the "Lifeline" from that particular chapter a reality in your own life. You can memorize these verses, put them on your mirror, in your locker at school, or on the dashboard of your car. Plant them any place where they can prompt you to remember the truth when you need it the most.

If you find *Some Assembly Required* helpful, you may want to study the rest of the *Lifelines* introductory series. They are:

No Pain, No Gain (Book 3)   Training for Spiritual Fitness

Warning: This Christian Is Highly Explosive! (Book 4)   Impacting the World Through Your Commitment to Christ

Still more Lifelines books are listed on the back cover of this book.

1

How Many Me's Are There Anyhow?

Opening Lines

Becoming a Christian was an exciting and really radical step for me. I felt truly sorry for my past sins. I was eager to begin living a new life in Christ.

My pre-Christian life had included the frequent use of alcohol and drugs. I had very little respect for authority and felt sympathetic toward all the "causes" of the sixties. So a real reconstruction had to take place in my heart when I handed it over to the Lord.

The way I had been living, and the new life that Jesus held forth were as different as black and white — no murky gray areas to grope my way through. And the fact that Jesus had saved me was such wonderful news that I wanted to tell the whole world.

I returned to the familiar places where my folk-rock group had performed — including several bars in our college town. Enthusiastically, I shared from the stage and among groups of old friends about the love of Jesus Christ and his offer of salvation.

But often, as I visited the night spots where I had so recently been "the life of the party," something very discouraging happened. It wasn't being rejected by old friends. I expected that. The enemy was me! Most of the time, instead of being a good

Christian influence on my old friends, I ended up being drunk by the end of the night! Needless to say, I felt ashamed and defeated.

What in the world was happening? I felt really depressed. Wasn't I supposed to be the one who possessed the truth? Wasn't I supposed to be the one who was now a brand new person in Christ? Wasn't I the one who had willingly and lovingly surrendered my life to Jesus Christ? How could I explain why I was so weak and susceptible to sin? How about you? Do you find yourself, as a Christian, doing things you know you shouldn't do? Things you don't even *want* to do? What's the story on this anyway?

On the Lines

1. Look up 2 Corinthians 5:17. How does this verse describe someone who is "in Christ" — a Christian, in other words?

_____

_____

2. Ezekiel 36:26 gives us some insight into just what exactly is *new* about a Christian. According to this verse, what is it?

_____

What do you think it means to have a "new heart?" Check as many as you think apply:

☐ new desires   ☐ new outlook

☐ new values   ☐ new lifestyle

☐ new personality   ☐ new appearance

☐ new talk   ☐ new direction

3. The Bible describes some of the things that should characterize this "new self" in Colossians 3:12-14. What are they?

_____

_____

_____

4. But the Bible speaks of *another* self, beside our new self, that
all Christians have. Look up Ephesians 4:22-24. What is this other
self?

_____

5. The Bible lists several types of behavior that characterize our
old self. I have to warn you that it's not a very attractive list. But if
we're honest with ourselves, we have to admit that it's accurate.
Look up Colossians 3:5-9 and Galatians 5:19-21. Note all the
characteristics of your old self that you can find listed there.

Characteristics Of My "Old Self"

_____   _____

_____   _____

_____   _____

_____   _____

_____   _____

_____   _____

6. Look up Galatians 5:16-17 and use what you read there to
answer this question: Does my old self go away when I become a
Christian? Explain.

_____

_____

_____

_____

_____

7. Think carefully as you answer this question: Is it possible that struggling with sin in your life is actually *evidence* that you *are* a Christian? Using what you have learned so far in this chapter, explain your answer.

_____

_____

_____

_____

_____

_____

Between the Lines

1. The fact of the matter is, if you are a Christian, you have *two* selves — the new and the old — both of which are very alive and active. In fact, they are actually "waging war" against each other all the time. What does God command you to do with this *old* self in Colossians 3:5? (Check the exact wording in the *New International Version.*)

_____

2. There are a number of ways something can be "put to death." You can shoot it, drown it, or poison it. But that type of approach won't work with your old self. Another way to kill something is to starve it. What might it mean to starve your old self?

_____

_____

_____

3. Look back at your list from question 5 in "On the Lines." What is one thing on that list that you see evident in your life?

_____

Write out below what it would take to *starve* that particular sin in your life.

_____

_____

_____

Would you be *willing* to starve that sin?

☐ yes   ☐ no

If you marked "yes," write out exactly *how* you plan to go about starving that sin.

_____

_____

_____

_____

_____

4. Is there a close friend of the same sex who could hold you accountable for your plan? It needs to be someone who will check up on you, and will let you know whether you are feeding or starving that sin. Call or get together with that person today and tell them what you want to do. Ask them if they would be willing to check up on your progress.

Closing Lines

Well, what was wrong with me back at the beginning of my Christian life? Why was I stumbling back to my dorm room drunk, after going out sober with a message that made life worth living? Why was my desire to share the gospel getting drowned in a sea of sin?

The problem was, I was trying to take my *new* self into my *old* world; I was feeding my old nature, and expecting my new nature to emerge as the winner.

Eventually, I realized that I was not yet strong enough to spend a lot of time with non-Christian friends — or even Christian friends who were weak in their faith. I cared about them, but couldn't resist the temptation to participate in their partying. I needed to *starve* my old self. And that was a *really* difficult thing to do. Physical starvation doesn't happen overnight, nor can we expect to starve sinful habits in a day. I loved those people and places. When I stopped going to the bars, some of my old friends reacted with ridicule. They said I thought that I was "too good for them." The truth of the matter was, I was not too good — I was too vulnerable — too easily lured into the old life.

The battle between our two selves is one of the toughest things in the Christian life. I've been a Christian for almost twenty years and the battle still rages. My old self will always crave sin. I can assure you that the sooner you start *putting to death* the things your old self desires, the easier the struggle will be. There *is* victory and we need to remind one another of that assurance. Christ has promised to help us through any temptation, but before we win we must admit there's a battle going on inside us. How about it? Why not declare war today!

Lifeline

I need to put on my new self, and declare war on my old self!

His Lines

Galatians 5:17

Colossians 3:1-3

The Bottom Line (For Group Discussion)

1. I often tell my students that the fight within them is actually evidence that they are spiritually alive. In fact, if there's *not* an internal struggle, it may indicate that they're *not* a Christian. Do you agree with that statement? Explain.

2. There's a bumper sticker that says, "Christians aren't perfect, just forgiven." Do you believe that is all there is to the issue? Explain. Do you think that Christians should display a bumper sticker like this to the watching world? Will non-Christians understand the message? Explain.

3. What are the most common ways that we "feed" our old self?

4. Often in speaking of a movie or album that we've watched or listened to, we tell people that "there are a few bad parts, but the rest is pretty good." How does this type of thinking hold up in light of what you've discovered in this chapter?

5. What are some ways to "feed" our new self? How is this group feeding your new selves? Your old selves?

2

The Crisis-of-the-Day Club

Opening Lines

Trevor is a deeply sensitive and caring guy. You'd love to have him for a friend — but you might often become impatient with him. You see, Trevor suffers from a chronic case of "postpone-itis." You know the kind. He lets things go until they reach crisis proportions, the crisis being the signal that forces Trevor to simply "get going." This happens on a daily basis, and includes the full range of his activities — term paper deadlines, baseball physicals, meeting someone for a movie, appointments with teachers (I'm speaking from personal experience here!).

Trevor *always* waits until the last minute. And invariably by that time it's too late. Now Trevor turns on his natural charm. With his big brown eyes he begs for mercy. "Just a few more days," or "just a few more minutes" — that's what Trevor always seems to need.

When Trevor was new to our school, teachers would surrender to his supposed sincerity and give in to his pleas. But after a persistent diet of his postpone-itis, teachers eventually became angry and callous toward Trevor's schemes.

Trevor was always late to my first-hour Bible class. He would fall in a few minutes after the bell had rung, with a steaming mug of coffee in hand. Then that winning smile would appear while he slowly slid into his seat. I guess I extended grace upon grace.

As the end of the year approached, Trevor's unfinished work warranted that he receive a "D" for my class. I wrestled with whether or not I should remind him that his work was not turned in. I had told all the seniors, three times, that Friday was the final deadline for late work. They knew that any assignments handed in after that date simply "didn't exist" as far as my grade book was concerned. I liked Trevor. We had become good friends and I had rescued him from failure before. I didn't want to simply let him "blow" his grade so close to graduation. But, I reasoned, somewhere along the line, Trevor's got to learn responsibility for himself.

Well, I decided *not* to say anything. Trevor received an "F" for the two missing assignments, which forced his existing "B" down to a "D" for the quarter. Needless to say, when grade cards were distributed, Trevor was devastated. This was a crisis that he hadn't planned for and couldn't postpone. It was too late. The red ink that recorded his "D" wouldn't wash away.

So what lesson is there for all of us in Trevor's story? What spiritual truth can we learn? We all have friends like Trevor. Perhaps Trevor's story is *your* story. Maybe not in school, but how about in your life as a Christian? Are you starting to miss appointments with God? Are you thinking you'll just go along at your own leisurely pace . . . until a crisis hits?

On the Lines

1. Write out the reasons why you went to the doctor the last three times:

Visit #1 _____

Visit #2 _____

Visit #3 _____

2. Were your visits to *prevent* something bad from happening to you, or were they because you were *already sick* and wanted to get well?

☐ preventive   ☐ needed to get well

3. These two different approaches to physical health can also show up in the way we look after our spiritual health. We can live our lives as we please, and when trouble comes, get serious with God; or, we can live in such a way that we are already prepared when hard times hit. Look at each verse below: if you think it best describes a preventive approach to spiritual health, mark a "P" next to it. If you think it best describes a crisis approach, mark a "C." (If it describes both approaches, mark it with both letters.)

_____Isaiah 1:15-16   _____Jeremiah 2:27

_____1 Peter 2:2   _____Matthew 25:1-13

_____Ephesians 6:11-18

4. If we always wait until we're sick to go to the doctor, then expect him to "fix" us, we can get into the habit of neglecting our physical health. What parallels or similarities do you see in terms of our spiritual health?

_____

_____

_____

_____

_____

5. What do you think are some of the key ingredients in staying physically healthy?

KEYS TO PHYSICAL HEALTH

_____

_____

_____

_____

_____

6. What do you think are the *spiritual* equivalents to your answers to question 5 above? In other words, what are the things that you think keep a person *spiritually* healthy? List them below.

KEYS TO SPIRITUAL HEALTH

_____

_____

_____

_____

Between the Lines

1. Chances are, perhaps without even meaning to, you have adopted a crisis approach to your life as a Christian, rather than one of preventive spiritual fitness. Don't get too discouraged. It's pretty common for that to happen, even to older Christians. But it's not terminal! You may be near death spiritually, but the Lord said, "A bruised reed he will not break, and a smoldering wick he will not snuff out" (Matthew 12:20). In fact, the rest of *Some Assembly Required* is dedicated to helping you become spiritually fit.

If you have tended to view God as a sort of spiritual Hotline — you know, when you're in deep trouble you dial 1-800-God-Help — then we'd like you to write the Lord a personal letter in the space provided. Tell him what you've discovered about your relationship with him and what you would like to see changed. It may seem a little strange to write a letter to God, but it's a concrete way to record your commitment. So . . . do it!

Dear God,

Closing Lines

Trevor graduated . . . but *barely.* His parents were stressed out, many teachers were hurt, and some felt angry. I got a phone call from Trevor in mid-summer, asking if I would write letters of recommendation for him because he was having a hard time getting into college! Most of his friends had been accepted at universities by early spring. But Trevor was just starting to get serious about finding a college a few weeks before school began!

Jill and I believe that Trevor will make it in life. He's beginning to get things together. In fact, he's even started to realize his need for some spiritual discipline. He purposely applied, and was accepted, at a college that "majors" on teaching people how to be spiritually fit.

It's so easy for us all to take a crisis approach to our Christian life. We think we can wing it. I mean, when things are going fine, who really needs God? "I'm doing fine without him," is our familiar attitude. But the truth is, God doesn't desire or appreciate this form of relationship. He's a person and wants you and me to work on cultivating a friendship with him, much like we do with each other. That means spending time with him, for starters. How would you feel if you had a friend who only called you when he needed money or was in trouble?

Fortunately, God is not impatient and easily hurt like we are. But the principle is the same. Spiritual fitness doesn't apply just to facing life's hassles; it's the foundation of a relationship with the God who saved you and wants to *know* you. (He wants you to desire his friendship more than just in the crisis times.) So . . . let's take a serious look at training for spiritual fitness.

Lifeline

God wants to be my friend in normal times as well as in crisis times.

His Lines

1 Timothy 4:7-8

Isaiah 29:13

The Bottom Line (For Group Discussion)

1. How can we help our friends in times of crisis so that we are genuine friends, but aren't taking the place of God as their source of strength?

2. Some have described the crisis approach to God as a pie chart in which he occupies one slice, and all the other areas of our life belong to us. Do you think this is accurate? Explain.

3. Contemporary songs and movies often suggest that it is good to be free of commitments to other people. Has this attitude affected Christians? Does it affect our willingness to be committed to each other? How about our commitment to God?

4. Do you think there is any relationship between our physical health and our spiritual health? Explain.

5. Have each member in the group share their answers to question 6 in "On the Lines" in order of importance, as they would rank them. Compare and discuss them.

6. If group members are willing, have them share examples from their lives of when they have taken a crisis approach to their spiritual health. What have the results been?

3
The Buck Stops Here!

Opening Lines

It was one of those yearned-for years when an athletic team has all the perfect touches to take the state tournament. Over the year our school had seen a basketball talent emerge among a handful of high school girls that has not since reappeared on the court. The entire starting team was outstanding in every area. They could dribble, shoot, steal, pass, and run flawlessly. Their season record showed it. They had advanced to the district tournament, the final "pit stop" in their seemingly inevitable race to the state championships in Denver. The atmosphere at the school was charged with anticipation. Visions of victory made the mood electric — even among the kids who didn't usually care about sports.

Finally, the long-awaited district tournament arrived. Buses and cars anxiously forged their way down the freeway to the first game. The game began and, from the first point on, the suspense had stomachs tied in knots. The score teetered back and forth as the clock erased the time. It was the final minutes of the fourth quarter and we were trailing by just two points. After a flurry of activity up and down the court and an error on the opponents' part, we tied the game. With only seconds remaining, our girls made a free throw which put us one point ahead. The victory seemed secure. The state tournament was only a heartbeat away. But then the other team brought the ball onto the court, the buzzer sounded, and at least two full seconds after the buzzer, one of their girls took a shot. The ball swished nicely through the net, but it was clearly too late to count . . .

Or so we thought! The head referee stepped confidently over to the score table, said the basket was good, spun around and walked off the court! The game was over, and due to this one man's decision, we *lost* the game that we had just won!

Our fans were stunned, our players devastated. Several parents from the *other* team even came forward and admitted that they were sorry about the ref's decision. It didn't seem fair, even to our opponents! As the tears were dried and the gym slowly emptied, we returned home reliving the ref's incompetence over and over again.

But, in the final analysis, as the referee, he was the final authority for the game. His word was what mattered, not our pleas nor our tears. Our feelings were real, and they were valid, but they didn't count. We felt like victims. But reality was that the ref gave the victory to the other team, and his word was final.

As a growing Christian, who or what is "ref" in *your* life? Is it your own feelings? Perhaps it's your own ideas or opinions? Is it your friends? Who or what "makes the calls" in your life? And . . . or . . . does it really matter?

On the Lines

1. Psalm 1:1-2 gives a sobering warning about who or what can be the "referees," the major influences on our thinking. Look at these verses, and write out below who or what are the possible referees for our life.

---

2. Look up the verses below, and write out who or what you think the "referee" was for this individual's life:

Exodus 5:2_____

1 Kings 12:6-11_____

2 Kings 18:1-6_____

3. Clearly, the most important referee or authority for the Christian is God's Word, the Bible. Look up the following verses and put into your own words what they each say about God's Word (or his teaching, or law).

Psalm 19:7. How is God's Word described?

_____

Matthew 4:4. How important is God's Word in our life?

_____

Psalm 119:89-93. God's Word was written in the past. Is it still relevant for today?

_____

Psalm 119:105. What is God's Word good for? (Think about what a lamp does.)

_____

John 8:31. Everyone seems to have opinions about how to live. What claim does Jesus make here about God's Word?

_____

Hebrews 4:12. In what sense does God's Word penetrate my life like a sword?

_____

4. In your own words, write out why you believe that God's Word must be the referee, the final authority in the life of the Christian.

_____

_____

_____

_____

_____

Between the Lines

1. Take a moment right now, and ask yourself the question, "Who or what has been the referee, or final authority in my life up until now?" Record your answer below.

☐ my ideas   ☐ my friends

☐ my Bible   ☐ my feelings

2. How would you rate your *willingness* to submit yourself to God's Word? Place a mark on the line below that accurately represents your heart at this point in your life.

_____

Obedient   Total
Servant   Rebel

3. Look over your answers to questions 1 and 2 above. Psalm 1 says that the man who loves the Lord and his Law is actually happy ("blessed" means happy). If you realize that God's Word needs to have more authority in your life, take a moment right now, bow your head and express that to the Lord. Ask him to use the rest of this study to give you specific direction on exactly *how* to make that happen. Be honest. Be courageous!

Closing Lines

That dismal night at the district game, an injustice took place that meant we lost the possibility of taking our team to state. But whether or not the ref was right or fair was really not the issue. His job was to judge the plays at that basketball game. Our feelings, our opinions, our disagreement with his decision didn't count for anything. Injustice is all around us. And we live in a day when we believe that our "rights" can be demanded. But in the final analysis, none of us is really free to be our own judge. Even people who don't believe that God exists will still one day give an account to him for what they have done with their lives. Why? Because he is God.

As Christians, you and I are under authority. Authority that is ultimately for our good. The question is: "Who or what is the authority in my life?" The proper answer for any believer is, God's Word. I tell my students with passion that, as Christians, if we discover that God's Word disagrees with our opinion, we are under obligation to *change* our opinion!

Next chapter we'll look at some practical ways to become familiar with God's Word so that it can indeed be your authority and your safety. But for now, we hope that you have chosen to make God's Word *your* referee. There's much more at stake than a state basketball game!

Lifeline

For Christians, the Bible is the final authority.

His Lines

Matthew 4:4

Joshua 1:8

The Bottom Line (For Group Discussion)

1. What is a Christian's responsibility when civil authority asks him to disobey the clear teaching of the Bible?

2. What is a Christian's responsibility when an employer asks him to disobey the clear teaching of the Bible?

3. Do you think there are "gray areas" in the Christian life — certain behavior that one Christian believes is wrong and another believes is permissible? In other words, are there things in the Bible that are not "black or white"?

Use the seven questions and Bible verses below as a springboard to evaluate any gray areas your group comes up with. (Anticipate a lively discussion!)

- Can God be glorified by this activity?
  (1 Corinthians 10:31)

- Is this a reflection of the "world's system"?
  (John 17:6)

- Is this something that Jesus would have done?
  (1 Peter 2:21)

- Would I be embarrassed to be doing this when Jesus returns? (1 John 2:28)

- Can I freely engage in this activity knowing that a holy God lives inside me? (1 Corinthians 6:19)

- Is this proper conduct for someone who calls himself a child of God? (2 Corinthians 5:17)

- Does this affect others in a negative way?
  (Romans 2:24)

4. Does a Christian have a better basis for truth than a nonbeliever, who has to rely upon his own ideas or those of others? Why or why not?

4

A Verse a Day Keeps the Devil Away

Opening Lines

Craig's parents had been career missionaries. He had spent a good part of his life on foreign shores in mission schools. Christian education was something that had been a part of his life since he could walk and talk. Craig came across to all the kids at our school as being very familiar with the Scriptures. He seemed to have accumulated a great deal of biblical knowledge in his eighteen years.

Very often Craig would be the first student to speak up in Senior Bible when I posed a difficult spiritual question for the class to ponder. On Mondays, the day I had set aside for prayer, Craig usually had a long list of things he wanted the class to pray about. He spoke often of various people he knew from work or church that he wanted to see become Christians. He told us how he was spending time with them, trying to help them grow spiritually.

I suppose seeing and hearing all of this day after day caused me to come to some very positive conclusions about Craig and his relationship with Jesus Christ. That is why I was so disillusioned when I discovered that Craig's close *friends* could paint quite a different portrait of this "man of God!" Apparently, Craig

33

was a wild drinker on the weekends, had a rather foul mouth, and used anger and intimidation to get his friends to see things his way. He was even exerting a negative influence on a number of guys from the public school who had just become Christians out of a loose lifestyle of drinking and drugs by showing them that Christians can "party hearty" too. Instead of being a "light in a dark place" for these new Christians, Craig was working hard to snuff out their flickering spiritual flame almost as quickly as it had ignited.

When he put forth his spiritual image each morning in Bible class, his friends saw it as nothing more than a masterpiece of theater, an *act*. In fact, some were so deeply offended by his double life that they came to talk to me about it in private. They said they felt like gagging, listening to him preach in class, knowing that his private life was quite another story.

How can someone who seems to know so much about Christ, Christianity, and the Bible, be so hypocritical? Is it possible for a person to get "into" God's Word but God's Word *not* get into them?

On the Lines

1. Psalm 119 in the Old Testament portion of the Bible contains 176 verses. You might be surprised to learn that *every one* of those 176 verses talks about God's Word! Below is a list of verses from Psalm 119 and a series of statements about God's Word. Match the Bible reference with the letter from the statement that you think best fits:

STATEMENTS ABOUT GOD'S WORD	VERSES FROM PSALM 119 ABOUT GOD'S WORD

A. I need to spend more time with *others* who love God's Word.   verse 11 _____

B. God's Word should be more important to me than money or possessions.   verse 18 _____

C. Memorizing God's Word can help
keep me from sinning.   verse 45 _____

D. I should think about what God
has said throughout the day.   verse 46 _____

E. I shouldn't be ashamed to share
God's Word with others.   verse 63 _____

F. God's Word can provide me with
guidance and direction for my life.   verse 72 _____

G. I should have a deep respect for God's Word.   verse 97 _____

H. I need God's help to understand the Bible.   verse 105 _____

I. God's Word can be a source of
comfort during hard times.   verse 120 _____

J. Obeying God's Word is a way to be truly free.   verse 143 _____

2. There are many ways to get God's Word "into" us. What are they? Draw a line connecting the verse on the left with the phrase on the right that tells how to get God's Word into your life.

Colossians 4:16   Memorize God's Word

Psalm 119:11   Study God's Word

Acts 17:11   Read God's Word

3. It's pretty obvious that God's Word is probably the most vital part of a Christian's spiritual health. But simply knowing the Bible isn't enough. What do the verses below have to say about your responsibility *to* God's Word?

1 Samuel 15:22 _____

Matthew 7:21 _____

John 14:23 _____

4. Go back to your answers to questions 1 and 2 above. Below, write out the two thoughts about God's Word from question 1 that struck you the most, and why.

Idea #1

_____

_____

_____

Idea #2

_____

_____

_____

Between the Lines

1. Look at your three answers to question 2. Which of the three do you feel is the weakest in your own life right now?

☐ reading   ☐ memorizing   ☐ studying

2. Tim Stafford, co-author of the *NIV Student Bible,* says that the three most common reasons that young people give for not spending more time in the Bible are:

☐ "I get discouraged because I can't seem to keep going consistently."

☐ "I can't understand it. It seems ancient and out of touch."

☐ "I can't find anything. I'm not familiar enough with it to be able to find anything."

Do any of these three apply to you? Which one does the most? Put a check in the box next to it?

3. The obvious truth is that we need help getting God's Word into us. A couple of the most basic helps are, having a *place* and a *plan*. If you don't already have a designated *place* where you can spend time reading and studying the Bible, that's the first thing you need to secure.

A place: Where, in your home, can you be alone and uninterrupted for fifteen to thirty minutes each day?

The second help is a *plan*. This doesn't have to be anything elaborate, simply a basic sense of direction for a limited time period on exactly *what* you're going to read, *why* you are reading it, and *how* you're going to go about it. Here's a suggestion:

A PLAN:

(1) *Read:* The passage assigned for each day (see the list below).

(2) *Write:* In a notebook, write out any thoughts about Jesus that struck you as you read.

(3) *Pray:* Ask God to make the characteristic of Jesus you saw real in your own life.

(4) *Memorize:* Try to find one verse for each week that means a lot to you. Write it out on a 3 x 5 card and work at memorizing it.

TWO WEEKS WITH THE SON OF GOD*

Day 1 — Luke 1:26-30	Getting ready for Jesus
Day 2 — Luke 2	The birth of Jesus
Day 3 — Mark 1	Jesus gets started

*Adapted from *The Student Bible, New International Version* © 1986 by The Zondervan Corporation. Used by permission.

Day 4 — Mark 9   A day with Jesus

Day 5 — Matthew 5   Jesus' most important sermon, part 1

Day 6 — Matthew 6   Jesus' most important sermon, part 2

Day 7 — Mark 15   Jesus the storyteller

Day 8 — John 3:1-21   An encounter at night

Day 9 — John 14   Jesus' last sermon

Day 10 — John 17   A prayer of Jesus

Day 11 — Matthew 26   Betrayed by a "friend"

Day 12 — Matthew 27   Crucifixion

Day 13 — John 20   Alive again!

Day 14 — Luke 24   A surprise guest

After you finish this project, try doing the same thing with the Book of Proverbs. There are thirty-one chapters — one for each day of the month. Or go to a local Christian bookstore and ask them what they have in the line of devotional books or guides for someone your age. The publication *Youthwalk* is available from Walk Thru The Bible Ministries, P. O. Box 80587, Atlanta, GA 30366. Subscription rates are $17 per year. It is an excellent devotional guide for young people, filled with relevant topics and how God's Word relates to them.

Closing Lines

Someone has said, "God's Word is intended to be a window into his very heart, but many Christians spend their entire lives merely polishing the glass." That was Craig. He had buckets of information about the Bible, but he didn't seem to have even a handful of personal knowledge about the God of the Bible. The facts *of* the Bible had never penetrated his heart and impacted his conduct. Craig had adopted a sort of "verse a day keeps the devil away" approach to his relationship with God.

God has given us his Word to let us know who he is and what he's like. We cannot decide for ourselves what he is like. If we love a person we will want to spend time with them. God wants us to spend time with him, listening and learning, but, the greatest goal of getting to know the Bible is that we *obey* it. Craig never made the connection, and his life clearly showed it. How are *you* doing?

Lifeline

It doesn't help to get into God's Word, unless God's Word gets into me!

His Lines

1 Samuel 15:22

James 1:22-25

The Bottom Line (For Group Discussion)

1. According to a recent Gallup Poll, the majority of Americans believe the Bible is divinely inspired, but only a small percentage of the same group could name four of the Ten Commandments. Do you think this is significant in light of this chapter? Explain.

2. Tim Stafford says, "The Bible is not a religious version of *Bartlett's Familiar Quotations,* providing raw material for greeting cards and bumper stickers" (*Campus Life,* July/August 1986, 48). What is he saying here? How does it relate to the truths you have learned in this chapter?

3. What would we be able to say and know about God if we didn't have the Bible? (An excellent way to demonstrate the necessity of God's Word is to stage a mock courtroom scene, and have people try to prove what God is like *without using the Bible*.)

4. Here's an interesting activity for your group: Conduct interviews at some public place in your city; ask people:

   a. Do you believe the Bible is inspired by God?

   b. Do you personally *follow* the Bible's teachings?

   c. When was the last time you read from the Bible?

Break up into interview teams of two. Record people's answers on a note pad or cassette recorder,* then report back to the group.

*If you want to use a recorder, make sure it is acceptable to the person you are interviewing.

5

The Heavenly Hot Line

Opening Lines

We were the original "Motley Crew." My Afro hairstyle was about the size of a basketball (and was the same color!). With my weight never peaking above 115 pounds, I could easily have passed for a human Tootsie Roll Pop. Jill drifted onto campus each day in her well-worn, well-faded blue jeans that had a huge sunrise scene on one side with many beads and threads. Her hair hung loosely at shoulder length, wispy and carefree.

Then there was our buddy Bruce. His hair fell somewhere midway down his back and he wore more leather than the average Brahma bull. I mean, this guy was wild — and weather changes didn't affect his choice of apparel. Daily he donned a suede mountain hat adorned with the remains of various life-forms. His matching suede jacket had long fringes hanging from the sleeves, so that when he lifted his arms he looked like a human bat. Leather bags and tiny bells hung from his hand-crafted belt, and his feet were destined to die inside a pair of dusty knee-high moccasins like Davey Crockett wore in the movies. We called him "Bummer" — a fitting title for this blossoming sixties renegade.

There were quite a few of us characters on campus whose descriptions were as Technicolored as Bummer's. The media christened us "Hippies" — we called ourselves "freaks."

About this time, God brought a man to our college campus who had a heart to share the gospel with young people. But Duane was almost as far removed from the hippie scene as one could get. He was what we called "straight." *Super* straight! Duane was a clean-cut Iowa farmer, with hair as short and straight as a toothbrush, who had come to our campus hungering to preach the gospel to a herd of humanoids who more closely resembled animated mops than people! We weren't your ideal congregation or potential youth group.

How could this one man, who on the surface appeared so "out-of-touch," ever get through to a group of know-it-all college students who honestly believed they were on the cutting edge of truth and reality? If you were Duane, what would *you* have done? As a matter of fact, what is the Christian's source of power when facing the impossible? What's the first thing *you* do when the going gets rough? When all the circumstances say *no hope?*

On the Lines

1. 1 Kings 18 shows us what our source of power should be as Christians. The story is about a power struggle between the false prophets of Baal and the true prophet of God. They decide on a way to determine which of their gods is really God.

Read 1 Kings 18:22-24. What exactly was to be the "contest"?

_____

_____

Look at verses 26-29. How did the false prophets try to win?

_____

_____

What did Elijah do? (verses 36-37)

_____

2. Prayer is the Christian's most powerful "weapon" when facing any difficulty. But, prayer is more than a weapon. Read Psalm 62:8. What phrase in this verse is describing prayer?

_____

What do you think this phrase means?

_____

_____

3. What promise concerning prayer do you see in the following verses?

    Isaiah 65:24 _____

    Psalm 91:15 _____

4. If God *promises* to answer prayer, then let's look at some of the ways he actually does. Read the verses below and match them with the answer (second column) that best fits (each answer is used only once):

VERSE   GOD'S ANSWER

1. ___ Judges 6:39-40   A. "Not yet!"

2. ___ Psalm 13:1   B. "No!"

3. ___ 2 Corinthians 12:8-9   C. "Yes!"

4. ___ Mark 14:32-36, 41-42   D. "No, because my will
                                                   demands something
                                                   'higher'."

5. Below are some things that cause God to say no when we pray. Look up the verse and write what you find on the appropriate "Barrier."

Psalm 66:18   James 4:3   Proverbs 21:13

6. Let's summarize. In the space below, check one thing under each heading that struck you the most in this chapter:

WHAT PRAYER IS

☐ a powerful weapon

☐ talking openly and honestly to God

☐ being honest with God is more important than a "proper sounding" prayer

ANSWERS TO PRAYER

☐ God hears before I even speak.

☐ No! is a valid answer to prayer. (God knows what is best for me even if I don't understand.)

☐ Not yet! is a valid answer to prayer. (Again, God knows best.)

☐ Yes . . . but not how you planned! is a valid answer to prayer.

☐ No, because I have a higher purpose! is a valid answer to prayer.

OBSTACLES TO ANSWERED PRAYER

☐ Secret sins can block my prayers.

☐ Selfish requests can block my prayers.

☐ Not caring about the needs of others can block my prayers.

Between the Lines

1. Which descriptions below best fit your present prayer life? Check as many as apply. Be honest!

☐ *Robin Hood*

You have a quiver full of short, "arrow" prayers that you shoot off to God whenever a crisis hits (e.g., failing a class, asking for a date, not getting in trouble).

☐ *The Jogger*

You almost always pray "on the run." You don't take time to pray regularly, so you do it when you're leaving the house, getting dressed, and of course . . . before meals.

☐ *The Coma Patient*

You end each day talking to God . . . or at least you *think* you do.

You're not totally sure because you faithfully fall off to sleep before you finish praying.

☐ *The Televangelist*

You pray best in public (at youth group, during family devotions, etc.), especially if there are other people listening, because you are really praying to impress them.

☐ *The Shopping-Spree Winner*

Your prayers consist primarily of long *lists* of things you want. Even your prayers for others have some personal benefit for you.

☐ *The Tax Collector* (See Luke 18:9-13.)

You pray honest prayers from the heart. You recognize that it is a privilege to have God listen at all. You are humble and reverent as you approach the Lord. You know that he really knows what is best for you and that he cares about every detail of your life.

2. Living in an age when international crises are "solved" on our TV in thirty minutes (and three commercials), taking *time* to pray seems a bit odd. Yet, it's God's method. It won't just "happen." It *is* work. In fact, prayer has been called the Christian's most important work. Below are a few suggestions on how to become more like *"The Tax Collector,"* described above:

FIND A PLACE where you will not be interrupted and could even talk to God aloud without being thought of as a mental case.

MAKE A PLAN. What do you want to pray about? Who do you want to pray for? When did God answer other prayers and how? Write down what's going on in your prayer life from time to time. You will see how God answers if you keep track of what you pray.

SET A TIME. *When* you pray is not as important as taking the time to do it. Start out with five to ten minutes. Find the time of day when you are most alert and can give full attention to what you're doing.

HAVE AN OPEN HEART. Expect God to answer when you talk to him. You'll be surprised at the things God brings to mind if you'll take him seriously. Pause and listen once in a while — you don't need to do all the talking!

READ. Find a good book on the subject of prayer and read it. Ask your pastor or youth worker to recommend one.

Closing Lines

Well, what do you think happened that year Duane took on the task of leading our campus counterculture to Christ? Surprise! There was a genuine spiritual revival among the "stoners" and "long hairs." The message of forgiveness in Jesus Christ spread like a flame through a dry field. Duane was sharing the gospel every time he turned around. The hippies who used to seek peace, parties, and protests, were actually excited about getting to know God and giving their lives to him. We would recruit a whole dorm full of our friends to listen to Duane explain God's plan of salvation. What had happened? How could this guy have gotten so in touch so fast?

Well, it turned out that, although Duane didn't have a handle on the hippie lifestyle, he did have a hot line to heaven. Duane knew the power of prayer. I can still recall an incident one evening shortly before I surrendered my life to Christ. The bars had just closed, it was about 1:00 A.M. I had to walk past Duane's house on the way back to my dorm. I cast a glance at his darkened house and noticed that a basement light was on. I figured he had forgotten to turn it off. But, you can already guess what Duane was doing at 1:00 A.M., can't you? He was down on his knees, praying for a bunch of foul-mouthed, cocky, carefree college students like me.

It was through the prayers of this one man, in touch with God, that the destinies of hundreds of students were changed forever. In fact, as you read this story and do this Bible study, you ought to stop and pray *right now.* Thank God for Duane. Because in reality, if it hadn't been for *his* commitment to pray, *you'd* be

doing something else at this very moment! In the words of one
Christian author:

> Men may spurn our appeals, reject our messages, oppose
> our arguments, despise our persons, but they are helpless
> against our prayers.
>
> J. Sidlow Baxter

Lifeline

Prayer unleashes the power of God.

His Lines

1 John 5:14

Luke 18:1

The Bottom Line (For Group Discussion)

1. Is there a difference between praying and "saying our
prayers"? Explain.

2. Why pray at all, if God already knows everything anyway?

3. How often does your group meet just to pray? Should you
make changes in this regard?

4. Meeting regularly with another person (sometimes called a
prayer partner), is an excellent way to be disciplined in prayer.
Discuss how members of your group could "pair off" to pray. Try
doing it for a three-month period.

5. The March/April 1988 issue of *Group* magazine has excellent
step-by-step instructions for planning a weekend retreat on the
theme of prayer. Secure a copy and start planning!

6

Stay Near the Fire!

Opening Lines

Kent's dad is a pastor. Preachers' kids ("PK's") are under constant pressure. Everyone seems to have superhuman expectations of them, and they know it. They are supposed to know and obey all the "shoulds" and "should nots."

One of my other students whose father is also a pastor confessed to me one day that she felt confined like a goldfish in a small bowl. When I questioned her further she explained, "It's like everybody is watching my whole life and I can't escape!"

I suppose Kent felt the same way. Many PK's resent all the rules they feel are put upon them. That's probably part of the reason he made the choice to hang out with a group of guys who were recognized rowdies. They were also very streetwise. Kent didn't *have* to make this choice. He was a star soccer player and could easily have become close with the guys on the team — after all, he was with them a lot.

Whatever the reason, Kent and his buddies cultivated a lifestyle that was far from the will of God. Weekend drinking became a regular routine for the group. Then, Kent's language slowly began to change. Soon, he found himself cursing the same Lord who had died for him. Finally, sexual temptations beckoned louder and louder. Chuck, Kent's closest "friend" in the group began to boast that he had cashed in his virginity. Consequently, Kent began to ponder if this was the next step in his own quest for individuality.

Kent was definitely a Christian. So, what was happening to him? Obviously his behavior was wrong. But *why* was he being sucked into the whirlpool of a degenerating lifestyle that ends in pain and destruction, sometimes even death?

What about you? Are you growing in your relationship with Jesus? Or, like Kent, are you trying to "swim the whirlpool"? If that's the case, this chapter's for you!

On the Lines

1. It is important to discover what it means to be a Christian in regard to your relationship with *other* Christians.

   • Look at Romans 8:15. What is God to *you,* if you are a Christian?

   _____

   • Now look at 2 Corinthians 6:18. What are you to *God,* if you are a Christian?

   _____

2. Christians share a special family relationship with each other. The Bible uses the word "fellowship" to describe this relationship. Below are some verses that speak of the *benefits* and *responsibilities* of fellowship. Look up each verse and think deeply about it. Then, write out what you think the verse teaches about your family relationships with other Christians.

Hebrews 10:24

My Thoughts:

_____

_____

_____

_____

Hebrews 10:25

My Thoughts:

_____

_____

_____

Ecclesiastes 4:9-10

My Thoughts:

_____

_____

_____

1 Corinthians 15:33   (The *New International Version* is best
                          on this one.)

My Thoughts:

_____

_____

_____

Hebrews 3:12-13

My Thoughts:

_____

_____

_____

_____

John 15:12

My Thoughts:

_____

_____

_____

_____

Acts 2:44-46

My Thoughts:

_____

_____

_____

_____

Between the Lines

1. Which two verses above meant the most to you and why?

Verse:

Why?

Verse

Why?

2. All of us have "primary" and "secondary" friends. The difference between them is:

PRIMARY FRIENDS

Their influence on *me* is greater or the same as my influence on them.

SECONDARY FRIENDS

My influence on *them* is greater or the same as their influence on me.

A Christian's primary friends should consist mostly of other committed Christians — believers who want to help each other grow. Their secondary friends can be composed both of Christians and non-Christians. How are *you* doing right now?

☐ My primary friends are mostly committed Christians.

☐ My primary friends are mostly non-Christians.

☐ My secondary friends are mostly non-Christians.

☐ My secondary friends are mostly Christians.

☐ My secondary friends are a mixture of Christians and non-Christians.

3. Are there any changes you need to make as a result of what you have learned in this chapter? Check the boxes below if they are changes you need to make right away:

☐ I have no close Christian friendships. I need to develop some.

☐ I need to break off some non-Christian friendships that I have.

☐ I need to develop some non-Christian secondary friendships.

☐ I need to spend more time with my Christian friends.

☐ I need to spend less time with my non-Christian friends.

☐ I need to find some Christian friends who are truly committed to Christ; some of the ones I have now aren't.

☐ I need to be a better friend to my Christian friends.

4. Write out below *what* you intend to do about this, *when* you intend to do it, and *how* you will go about it:

What I intend to do:

_____

_____

_____

When I intend to do it:

_____

How I intend to do it:

_____

_____

_____

Closing Lines

About the time Kent was pondering the value of his virginity, God brought our paths together. I began to keep him after class for a few minutes from time to time, just to gab. Slowly, he began to open up and tell me his story. I asked him tons of questions to help him come to terms with what was happening to him, what he *really* wanted out of life, and what he needed to do.

Kent made some new choices. Hard choices. To begin with, he broke off his "friendship" with Chuck. Then he began to cultivate friendships with other guys whose values and goals were in line with his own. Kent has slowly recovered the lost ground he surrendered. Right now he's growing as a Christian and doing fine.

Let me pass on to you a story from one of my many after-class conversations with Kent: "Kent," I said, "I was camping with my two young sons last weekend. As we sat around the fire, staring into the dancing flames, an ember popped out and landed by my feet. I told my two boys to watch it closely. They did. Then I asked them, 'What's happening to the ember?' They both replied, 'It's going out.' And I told them: 'That's what happens to Christians who get away from other Christians.'"

As I finished the story, I turned to Kent, poked his chest playfully and asked, "Get the point?"

Smiling, he said without hesitation, "Got it."

Do *you* get the point?

Lifeline

To survive, I need strong Christian friends.

His Lines

Ecclesiastes 4:9-10

Hebrews 10:24

The Bottom Line (For Group Discussion)

1. How can I be successful in developing friendships with people who haven't yet become followers of Christ? (Note: This assignment could be presented to your group in a panel discussion or "talk show" format where people share successes and failures.)

2. When should a Christian break off a friendship with a nonbeliever?

3. What is your group doing to reach nonbelievers?

4. Would you be embarrassed, or proud, to bring a nonbeliever to your group? Explain.

5. Have you ever thought that it's possible to have "fellowship" with the nonbelieving world through the media (e.g., music, movies, MTV)? In other words, can these things affect us like a Saturday night date might? Explain. If so, how do the principles of this chapter apply, if at all?